How Do You Say *Stomach* in Guatemala?

My List of Key Medical Terms In Spanish

José Luis Leyva

Copyright © 2015 José Luis Leyva

All rights reserved

Idea Editorial – www.ideaeditorial.com

ISBN: 1508471924
ISBN-13: 978-1508471929

PREFACE

This book will be very useful for healthcare professionals to learn just the key medical terms in Spanish. Rather than a thick dictionary, filled with explanations and multiple entries, ***How Do You Say Stomach in Guatemala?*** is a handy book that can be used when doing medical work in Guatemala. Get acquainted with the most common medical terms in Spanish.

ENGLISH-SPANISH
INGLÉS-ESPAÑOL

A

abdomen, abdomen
abdominal, abdominal
abnormal, anormal
abortion, aborto
abrasion, abrasión/raspadura
abscess, absceso
abstinence, abstinencia
abuse, abuso
accident, accidente
acetaminophen, acetaminofén
ache, dolor
acid, ácido
acne, acné
active, activo

My List of Key Medical Terms In Spanish

acute, agudo
addict, adicto
addiction, adicción
admit (into hospital), ingresar
adolescence, adolescencia
adopt (to), adoptar
adult, adulto
adrenaline, adrenalina
advise (to), aconsejar
afterbirth, placenta
agitation, agitación
ailment, enfermedad
air, aire
alcoholism, alcoholismo
alive, vivo
allergic, alérgico
allergy, alergia
ambulance, ambulancia
amenorrhea, amenorrea
amino acid, aminoácido
ammonia, amoníaco
amnesia, amnesia
amniocentesis, amniocentesis
amniotic sac, bolsa amniótica

amphetamines, anfetaminas
amputate (to), amputar
analgesic, analgésico
analysis, análisis
anaphylactic, shock anafiláctico
anatomy, anatomía
anemia, anemia
anemic, anémico
anesthesia, anestesia
anesthesiologist, anestesiólogo
aneurysm/aneurism, aneurisma
anger, enojo
angiogram, angiograma
angioplasty, angioplastia
anorexia, anorexia
antacid, antiácido
anthrax, ántrax
antibiotic, antibiótico
antibodies, anticuerpos
anticoagulant, anticoagulante
antidepressant, antidepresivo
antidote, antídoto
antihistamine, antihistamínico
anus, ano

My List of Key Medical Terms In Spanish

anxiety, ansiedad
aorta, aorta
apathy, apatía
apnea, apnea
appendectomy, apendectomía
appendicitis, apendicitis
appetite, apetito
applicator, aplicador
appointment, cita
arm, brazo
arm pit, axila
arrhythmia, arritmia
artery, arteria
arthritis, artritis
asphyxia, asfixia
asthma, asma
asthmatic, asmático
astigmatism, astigmatismo
athlete's foot, pie de atleta
atrophy, atrofia
autism, autismo
autopsy, autopsia
awake, despierto
awaken (to), despertar

B

baby, bebé
back, espalda
backbone, columna vertebral
bacteria, bacteria
bad, malo(a)
balance, equilibrio
bald, calvo
baldness, calvicie
bandage, vendaje
bandaid, curita
barbiturates, barbitúricos
barium, bario
basin, palangana
bath, baño

My List of Key Medical Terms In Spanish

bathe (to), bañarse
bed, cama
bedpan, orinal
bedridden (patient), encamado
bed-wetting, enuresis
behavior, conducta
belch, eructo
belly, vientre
bellybutton, ombligo
benign, benigno
bib, babero
biceps, bíceps
bicuspid, bicúspide
bile, bilis
bilirubin, bilirrubina
biological, biológico
biopsy, biopsia
birth, nacimiento/parto
birthmark, lunar
bite, mordedura
bite (insect), picadura
bitter, amargo
blackheads, espinillas
bladder, vejiga

bleed, sangrar

blind, ciego

blindness, ceguera

blink, parpadear

blister, ampolla

blockage, obstrucción

blood, sangre

body, cuerpo

bone, hueso

booster shot, vacuna de refuerzo

bottle, botella

botulism, botulismo

bowel, intestino

brace, aparato ortopédico

braces (dental), frenos dentales

brain, cerebro

break, quebrar

breast/chest, pecho/seno

breastbone, esternón

breath, aliento

breathe, respirar

broken, roto

bronchitis, bronquitis

bruise, moretón

My List of Key Medical Terms In Spanish

bruised, amoratado

bulimia, bulimia

bulimic, bulímico

bump, protuberancia

bunion, juanete

burn, quemadura

burp, eructar

bursitis, bursitis

buttock, glúteo

buzzing, zumbido

C

calcified, calcificado
calcium, calcio
calf (of leg), pantorilla
callus, callo
calorie, caloría
cancer, cáncer
cancerous, canceroso
cane, bastón
capillary, capilar
capsule, cápsula
carbohydrate, carbohidrato
carcinogenic, carcinogénico
carcinoma, carcinoma
cardiac, cardíaco

My List of Key Medical Terms In Spanish

cardiologist, cardiólogo

cardiology, cardiología

care, cuidado

cartilage, cartílago

cast, yeso

castration, castración

cataract, catarata

catatonic, catatónico

catheter, catéter

catheterization, cateterismo

catheterize, cateterizar

cause, causa

cauterize, cauterizar

cervix, cuello del útero

chafe, rozar

checkup, examen

cheek, mejilla

chemical, químico

chemotherapy, quimioterapia

chest, pecho

chew, masticar

chicken pox, varicela

childbirth, parto

childhood, infancia

chills, escalofríos
chin, barbilla
chiropractor, quiropráctico
chlamydia, clamidia
choke, ahogarse
cholera, cólera
cholesterol, colesterol
chronic, crónico
cigarette, cigarrillo
circulation, circulación
circumcision, circuncisión
cirrhosis, cirrosis
claustrophobia, claustrofobia
cleft palate, paladar hendido
clinic, clínica
clitoris, clítoris
clot, coágulo
cocaine, cocaína
coccyx, cóccix
codeine, codeína
cold, frío/a
cold (illness), resfriado común
cold sores, herpes labial
colic, cólico

My List of Key Medical Terms In Spanish

colitis, colitis
collagen, colágeno
collarbone, clavícula
colon, colon
colonoscopy, colonoscopía
color-blindness, daltonismo
colostomy, colostomia
coma, coma
comatose, comatoso
comfortable, cómodo
complaint, queja
complexion, tez
complication, complicación
compress, compresa
conceive, concebir
concussion, conmoción cerebral
condom, condón
confused, confundido
confusion, confusión
congenital, congénito
congested (to be), estar congestionado
congestion, congestión
conjunctiva, conjuntiva
conjunctivitis, conjuntivitis

*How Do You Say **Stomach** in Guatemala?*

conscious, consciente

consciousness, conocimiento

consent, consentir

constipation, estreñimiento

contagious, contagioso

contaminated, contaminado

contraception, anticoncepción

contractions, contracciones

contusion, contusión

convalescent, convaleciente

convulsion, convulsión

corn (callus), callo

coronary, coronario

cortisone, cortisona

cough, tos

cough, toser

CPR, reanimación cardiopulmonar

crabs, ladillas

cramp, calambre

cramps (menstrual), cólicos menstruales

cranium, cráneo

craving, antojo

crawl, gatear

crib, cuna

cripple, lisiar

crippled, lisiado

critical, crítico

Crohn's disease, enfermedad de Crohn

cross-eyed, bizco

croup, crup

crutches, muletas

cry, llorar

CT scan, tomografía por computadora

culture, cultivo

cure, curar

cut, cortar

cuticle, cutícula

cyst, quiste

cystic fibrosis, fibrosis quística

D

daily, diariamente
dandruff, caspa
danger, peligro
daze, aturdimiento
dead, muerto
deaf, sordo
deaf-mute, sordomudo
deafness, sordera
death, muerte
deceased, difunto
decongestant, descongestionante
defecate, defecar
defibrillation, desfibrilación
defibrillator, desfibrilador

My List of Key Medical Terms In Spanish

deficiency, deficiencia
deformed, deformado
deformity, deformidad
dehydration, deshidratación
delirious, delirante
delirium, delirio
delivery (of a baby), parto
deltoids, deltoides
dementia, demencia
dental, dental
dentist, dentista
denture, dentadura postiza
depigmentation, despigmentación
depression, depresión
dermatitis, dermatitis
dermatologist, dermatólogo
deterioration, deterioro
detoxification, desintoxicación
develop, desarrollar
diabetes, diabetes
diagnose, diagnosticar
diagnosis, diagnóstico
dialysis, diálisis
diaper, pañal

diaphragm, diafragma

diarrhea, diarrea

die, morir

diet, dieta

dietitian, dietista

digest, digerir

digestion, digestión

dilated, dilatado

dilation, dilatación

dilute, diluir

diphtheria, difteria

disability, discapacidad

discharge, secreción

discharge from hospital, dar de alta

discontinue, suspender

disease, enfermedad

disinfect, desinfectar

disinfectant, desinfectante

disk (slipped), disco desplazado

dislocation, dislocación

disorder, trastorno

disorientation, desorientación

distend, distender

distressed, angustiado

My List of Key Medical Terms In Spanish

diuretic, diurético
dizziness, mareos
dizzy, mareado
doctor, médico
doctor's office, consultorio
donor, donante
dosage, dosis
double vision, vista doble
drain, supurar
draw blood, sacar sangre
dropper, gotero
drops, gotas
drowning, ahogamiento
drowsy, somnoliento
drug addiction, adicción a las drogas
drugs (usually illicit), drogas
drugs (legal), medicinas
drunk, borracho
dryness, sequedad
due date, fecha aproximada de parto
dull (pain), sordo (dolor)
duodenum, duodeno
dust, polvo
dwarfism, enanismo

How Do You Say *Stomach* in Guatemala?

dysentery, disentería

dyslexia, dislexia

dystrophy, distrofia

E

ear (inner), oído

ear (middle), oído medio

ear (outer), oreja

earache, dolor de oído

eardrum, tímpano

earlobe, lóbulo

earplugs, tapones para los oídos

eczema, eccema

edema, edema

egg, huevo/óvulo

ejaculate, eyacular

EKG, electrocardiograma

elbow, codo

elderly, anciano

How Do You Say *Stomach* in Guatemala?

electrocardiogram, electrocardiograma

electrocution, electrocución

elixir, elixir

emaciated, escuálido

embolism, embolia

embryo, embrión

emergency, emergencia

pulmonary emphysema, enfisema pulmonar

encephalitis, encefalitis

endemic, endémico

endocrine, endocrino

endocrinologist, endocrinólogo

endorphin, endorfina

endoscopy, endoscopía

enema, enema

enlargement, agrandamiento

enzyme, enzima

epidemic, epidémico/epidemia

epidural, epidural

epiglottis, epiglotis

epilepsy, epilepsia

erection, erección

esophagus, esófago

estrogen, estrógeno

ether, éter

euphoria, euforia

Eustachian tube, trompa de Eustaquio

euthanasia, eutanasia

exam, examen

examine, examinar

excrement, excremento

exercise, ejercicio

exertion, esfuerzo

exfoliation, exfoliación

exhale, exhalar

exhaustion, agotamiento

expectorant, expectorante

expert, experto

explain, explicar

exposure, exposición

external, externo

extract, extraer

extraction, extracción

eye, ojo

eyebrow, ceja

eyelash, pestaña

eyelid, párpado

eyesight, vista

F

face, cara
face down, boca abajo
face up, boca arriba
faint, desmayarse
fainting spells, desmayos
fall, caída
Fallopian tubes, trompas de Falopio
false teeth, dientes postizos
family planning, planificación familiar
fast, ayunar
fat (food), grasa
fat (person), gordo
fatal, fatal/mortal
fatigue, fatiga

My List of Key Medical Terms In Spanish

fear, miedo

feces, heces

feed, alimentar

feel, sentir

feet, pies

femur, fémur

fertile, fértil

fertilization, fertilización

fetal monitor, monitor fetal

fetus, feto

fever, fiebre

fiber, fibra

fibrillation, fibrilación

filling (dental), empaste

finger, dedo (de la mano)

finger pad, yema

fire, fuego/incendio

first aid, primeros auxilios

fissure, fisura

fist, puño

flake, escama

flat foot, pie plano

flatulence, flatulencia

flexible, flexible

How Do You Say *Stomach* in Guatemala?

flu, gripe
fluoride, fluoruro
flush, rubor
foam, espuma
folic acid, ácido fólico
folk healer, curandero
follicle, folículo
follow-up, examen de seguimiento
food, alimentos
foot, pie
forceps, fórceps
forearm, antebrazo
forehead, frente
foreskin, prepucio
form, formulario
formula, fórmula
fracture, fractura
freckle, peca
freeze, congelar
frequency, frecuencia
fright, susto
function, función
fungus, hongo

G

gag, provocar náuseas

gain weight, subir de peso

gall bladder, vesícula biliar

gallstones, cálculos biliares

gangrene, gangrena

gargle, hacer gárgaras

gas, gas

gash, tajo

gastric ulcer, úlcera gástrica

gastritis, gastritis

gastroenterologist, gastroenterólogo

gastrointestinal (GI), gastrointestinal

gauze, gasa

gel, gel

How Do You Say *Stomach* in Guatemala?

gender, sexo

genes, genes

genetic, genético

genitals, genitales

geriatric, geriátrico

germ, germen

German measles, rubéola

gestation, gestación

gigantism, gigantismo

giardia, giardia

gingivitis, gingivitis

gland, glándula

glasses, gafas

glaucoma, glaucoma

glove, guante

glucose, glucosa

gluten, gluten

goiter, bocio

gonorrhea, gonorrea

goose bumps, piel de gallina

gout, gota

gown, bata

graft, injerto

gram, gramo

My List of Key Medical Terms In Spanish

grief, pesar

grieve, afligirse

grind, moler

groin, ingle

growth, crecimiento

guilt, culpa

gums, encías

gun, pistola

gurney, camilla

gut, intestino/tripas

gynecologist, ginecólogo

gynecology, ginecología

H

habit, hábito
hair, pelo
hair (body), vello
halitosis, mal aliento
hallucination, alucinación
hammer, martillo de reflejos
hamstring, músculo posterior del muslo
hand, mano
hangnail, padrastro
hangover, resaca
hardening, endurecimiento
harm, dañar
harmful, dañino
harmless, inofensivo

My List of Key Medical Terms In Spanish

head, cabeza
headache, dolor de cabeza
heal, curarse
health, salud
health care, atención a la salud
healthy, sano
hear, oír
hearing, audición
heart, corazón
heart attack, ataque cardíaco
heartbeat, latido del corazón
heartburn, acidez estomacal
heat-stroke, insolación
heating pad, cojín eléctrico
heel, talón
height, altura
helicopter, helicóptero
hematoma, hematoma
hemoglobin, hemoglobina
hemophilia, hemofilia
hemorrhage, hemorragia
hepatitis, hepatitis
herb, hierba
herbalist, yerbero

How Do You Say *Stomach* in Guatemala?

hereditary, hereditario

heredity, herencia

hermaphrodite, hermafrodita

hernia, hernia

heroin, heroína

herpes, herpes

heterosexual, heterosexual

hiccups, hipo

high blood pressure, presión alta

hip, cadera

hives, ronchas

hoarse, ronco

hoarseness, ronquera

homeopathy, homeopatía

homosexual, homosexual

hookworm, anquilostomosis

hormonal, hormonal

hormone, hormona

hospital, hospital

hospitalize, internar

hot flashes, sofocos

hunchback, jorobado

hurt, doler

hydrate, hidratar

My List of Key Medical Terms In Spanish

hydrogen peroxide, peróxido de hidrógeno

hygiene, higiene

hymen, himen

hyperactive, hiperactivo

hyperglycemia, hiperglucemia

hypersensitivity, hipersensibilidad

hypertension, presión alta

hyperthermia, hipertermia

hyperthyroidism, hipertiroidismo

hyperventilation, hiperventilación

hypochondria, hipocondria

hypoglycemia, hipoglucemia

hypothalamus, hipotálamo

hypothermia, hipotermia

hypothyroidism, hipotiroidismo

hypoxia, hipoxia

hysterectomy, histerectomía

hysteria, histeria

I

ibuprofen, ibuprofeno
ill, enfermo
illness, enfermedad
immature, inmaduro
immobile, inmóvil
immobilization, inmovilización
immune, inmune
immunize, inmunizar
impacted tooth, diente impactado
impaired, dañado
impairment, incapacidad
implant, implantar
impotence, impotencia
impregnation, fecundación

My List of Key Medical Terms In Spanish

incest, incesto

incision, incisión

incontinence, incontinencia

incubator, incubadora

incurable, incurable

indigestion, indigestión

induce, inducir

infant, bebé

infect, infectar

infection, infección

infertile, estéril

infertility, infertilidad

inflammation, inflamación

influenza, gripe

ingest, ingerir

inhale, inhalar

inhaler, inhalador

inject, inyectar

injury, lesión

inoculate, inocular

inoculation, inoculación

insane, loco

insanity, locura

insemination, inseminación

How Do You Say *Stomach* in Guatemala?

insomnia, insomnio

instrument, instrumento

insulin, insulina

insurance, seguro

intensive care, terapia intensiva

intercourse, relaciones sexuales

internal, interno

internist, internista

intestine, intestino

intoxication, intoxicación

intravenous fluids, líquidos intravenosos

intubation, intubación

iodine, yodo

iron, hierro

irregular heartbeat, latidos cardíacos irregulares

irrigate, irrigar

irritation, irritación

itch, comezón

J

jaundice, ictericia/piel amarilla

jaw, mandíbula

jelly, jalea

jock itch, tiña crural

joint, articulación

jugular, yugular

juice, jugo

K

kidney, riñón
kidney failure, insuficiencia renal
kidney stones, cálculos renales
knee, rodilla
kneecap, rótula
knife, cuchillo
knot, nudo
knuckle, nudillo

L

labor, trabajo de parto
labor pains, dolores de parto
laboratory, laboratorio
labyrinthitis, laberintitis
laceration, laceración
lactation, lactancia
lactose, lactosa
lame extremity, extremidad lisiada
language, lenguaje
laparoscopy, laparoscopía
large intestine, intestino grueso
laryngitis, laringitis
larynx, laringe
laser treatment, tratamiento con láser

latex, látex

laughing gas, gas hilarante (óxido nitroso)

laxative, laxante

lead, plomo

leech, sanguijuela

left-handed, zurdo

leg, pierna

leprosy, lepra

lesbian, lesbiana

lesion, lesión

lethargy, letargo

leukemia, leucemia

libido, deseo sexual

lice, piojos

life, vida

lifestyle, estilo de vida

ligament, ligamento

light-headedness, vahído

limb, extremidad

liniment, linimento

liposuction, liposucción

lips, labios

liquid, líquido

lisp, ceceo

My List of Key Medical Terms In Spanish

listen, escuchar

live, vivir

liver, hígado

lobe, lóbulo

lobotomy, lobotomía

lockjaw, tétanos

low blood pressure, presión baja

lozenges, pastillas para la garganta

lubricate, lubricar

lump, bulto

lumpectomy, tumorectomía

lungs, pulmones

lupus, lupus

lymph, linfa

lymph nodes, ganglios linfáticos

lymphoma, linfoma

M

malabsorption, malabsorción

malaise, malestar

malaria, paludismo

male, varón/masculino

malformation, malformación

malignant, maligno

malnutrition, desnutrición

malpractice, negligencia médica

mammogram, mamografía

mania, manía

manic-depressive, maníaco depresivo

marijuana, marihuana

mask, máscara

mass, masa

My List of Key Medical Terms In Spanish

massage/rub, masajear

mastectomy, mastectomía

maternal, materno

maturity, madurez

measles, sarampión

medical record, expediente médico

medication, medicamento

medicine, medicina

melanoma, melanoma

meningitis, meningitis

menopause, menopausia

menses, menstruación

menstrual cycle, ciclo menstrual

menstruation, menstruación

mental illness, trastorno mental

metabolism, metabolismo

metastasis, metástasis

methadone, metadona

methamphetamine, metanfetamina

microscope, microscopio

microsurgery, microcirugía

midwife, partera

migraine, migraña

mind, mente

How Do You Say *Stomach* in Guatemala?

miscarriage, aborto natural

mite, ácaro

mole, lunar

monitor, monitor

mononucleosis, mononucleosis

morgue, morgue

morphine, morfina

mortality, mortalidad

mouth, boca

mucous, mucoso/mucosa

mumps, paperas

muscle, músculo

mutation, mutación

mute, mudo

myopia, miopía

N

nail, uña

naked, desnudo

nap, siesta

nape, nuca

narcolepsy, narcolepsia

narcotic, narcótico

natural, natural

nausea, náuseas

navel, ombligo

nearsightedness, miopía

neck, cuello

needle, aguja

nerve, nervio

nervous, nervioso

neuralgia, neuralgia

neurologist, neurólogo

neurology, neurología

neurosis, neurosis

neurotic, neurótico

nicotine, nicotina

nightmare, pesadilla

nipple, pezón

nitroglycerine, nitroglicerina

normal, normal

nose, nariz

nostril, fosa nasal

nourishment, nutrición

numbness, adormecimiento

nurse, enfermera

nutrient, nutriente

nutrition, nutrición

nutritionist, nutricionista

O

obese, obeso

obesity, obesidad

obstetrician, obstetra

obstetrics, obstetricia

obstruction, obstrucción

occlusion, oclusión

odor, olor

office, consultorio

ointment, ungüento

oncologist, oncólogo

oncology, oncología

operate, operar

ophthalmologist, oftalmólogo,

optic, óptico

optometrist, optometrista
oral, oral
organ, órgano
orgasm, orgasmo
orthodontist, ortodoncista
orthopedics, ortopedia
orthopedist, ortopedista
osteoarthritis, osteoartritis
osteopath, osteópata
osteoporosis, osteoporosis
ovary, ovario
overdose, sobredosis
overweight, sobrepeso
ovulate, ovular
ovulation, ovulación
oxygen, oxígeno

P

pacemaker, marcapaso

pacifier, chupete

pain, dolor

pain reliever, calmante para el dolor

painful, doloroso

palate, paladar

pale, pálido

paleness, palidez

palpitations, palpitaciones

pancreas, páncreas

Pap smear, examen de Papanicolaou

paralysis, parálisis

paralyzed, paralítico

paramedic, paramédico

How Do You Say *Stomach* in Guatemala?

paranoia, paranoia

paraplegic, parapléjico

parasite, parásito

patch, parche

paternal, paterno

pathologist, patólogo

patient, paciente

pediatric, pediátrico

pediatrician, pediatra

pediatrics, pediatría

pelvis, pelvis

penetrate, penetrar

penicillin, penicilina

penis, pene

perforation, perforación

perspire, transpirar

pertussis, tos ferina

pharmacist, farmacéutico

pharmacy, farmacia

pharynx, faringe

phlegm, flema

phobia, fobia

phosphorus, fósforo

photosensitivity, fotosensibilidad

My List of Key Medical Terms In Spanish

physical therapy, fisioterapia

physician, médico

pill, píldora

pillow, almohada

pimples, espinillas

placenta, placenta

plague, plaga

plaque, placa

plasma, plasma

platelets, plaquetas

pneumonia, pulmonía

podiatrist, podólogo

poison, veneno

polio, poliomielitis

pollen, polen

polyp, pólipo

pore, poro

postmenopausal, postmenopáusico

post-op, después de la operación

postpartum, posparto

potassium, potasio

pound, libra

powder, polvo

predispose, predisponer

preeclampsia, pre eclampsia
pregnancy, embarazo
pregnant, embarazada
premature birth, nacimiento prematuro
premenopausal, pre menopáusico
prenatal care, cuidado prenatal
prescribe, recetar
prescription, receta
pressure, presión
prevent, prevenir
prevention, prevención
procedure, procedimiento
proctologist, proctólogo
progesterone, progesterona
prognosis, pronóstico
prostate gland, próstata
protein, proteína
psoriasis, psoriasis
psychiatrist, psiquiatra
psychologist, psicólogo
psychosis, psicosis
psychotherapy, psicoterapia
psychotic, psicótico
puberty, pubertad

My List of Key Medical Terms In Spanish

pubic hair, vello púbico

pulmonary, pulmonar

pulmonary edema, edema pulmonar

pulsating, pulsante

pulse, pulso

pump, bomba

pupil, pupila

pus, pus

Q

quadriceps, cuádriceps

quarantine, cuarentena

quinine, quinina

quota, cuota

R

rabies, rabia

radiation treatment, tratamiento de radiación

radiologist, radiólogo

radiology, radiología

radiotherapy, radioterapia

rape, violación

rash, erupción

reaction, reacción

reconstruct, reconstruir

recovery, recuperación

rectum, recto

redness, enrojecimiento

refill, rellenar

reflex, reflejo

How Do You Say *Stomach* in Guatemala?

reflux, reflujo

regurgitation, regurgitación

rehabilitate, rehabilitar

rehydrate, rehidratar

reject, rechazar

relapse, recaída

relationship (family), parentesco

relax, descansar

relief, alivio

remedy, remedio

renal failure, insuficiencia renal

replace, reemplazar

reproduce, reproducir

reproduction, reproducción

respirator, respirador

respiratory, respiratorio

rest, descansar

result, resultado

resuscitation, resucitación

retention, retención

retina, retina

revive, reanimarse

rheumatic fever, fiebre reumática

rheumatism, reumatismo

My List of Key Medical Terms In Spanish

rhinoplasty, rinoplastia

rhythm method, método del ritmo

rib, costilla

rigidity, rigidez

rigor mortis, rigor mortis

risk, riesgo

rubella, rubéola

runny nose, secreción nasal

rupture, ruptura

S

safe, seguro
saline, salino
saliva, saliva
salmonella, salmonela
salt, sal
sample, muestra
sane, cuerdo
sanitary, sanitario
sanity, cordura
sarcoma, sarcoma
scab, costra
scabies, sarna
scald, escaldadura
scale, balanza

My List of Key Medical Terms In Spanish

scalp, cuero cabelludo
scaly, escamoso
scar, cicatriz
scarlet fever, fiebre escarlatina
schizophrenia, esquizofrenia
sciatica, ciática
scissors, tijeras
scoliosis, escoliosis
scratch, rasguño
scream, grito
screen, examen de detección
scrotum, escroto
scurvy, escorbuto
sealant, sellador
seasickness, mareo (en un barco)
secrete, secretar
secretion, secreción
sedative, sedante
sedentary, sedentario
seizures, convulsiones
semen, semen
senile, senil
senility, senilidad
sensation, sensación

sensitive, sensible

sensitivity, sensibilidad

septum, tabique

serious, serio

serum, suero

severe, severo

sex, sexo

sexuality, sexualidad

shakes, temblores

sharp (pain), agudo (dolor)

shin, espinilla

shingles, herpes zoster

shiver, escalofríos

shiver, tiritar

shock, choque

shot, inyección

shoulder, hombro

shoulder blade, omóplato

sibling, hermano/hermana

sick, enfermo

sickness, enfermedad

side, lado

side effect, efecto secundario

sight, vista

My List of Key Medical Terms In Spanish

sinus, seno paranasal
sinusitis, sinusitis
skeleton, esqueleto
skin, piel
skinny, flaco
skull, cráneo
sleep, dormir
sleeping pill, somnífero
sleepy, tener sueño
sling, cabestrillo
slip, resbalar
slipped disc, disco desplazado
sliver, astilla
slur, arrastrar las palabras
small intestine, intestino delgado
smallpox, viruela
smell, oler
smoke, fumar
snakebite, mordedura de serpiente
sneeze, estornudar
snore, roncar
soap, jabón
sober, sobrio
social worker, trabajador social

How Do You Say *Stomach* in Guatemala?

sodium, sodio

sole (of foot), planta del pie

sonogram, ecografía

sore, llaga

spasm, espasmo

specialist, especialista

specimen, muestra/espécimen

speculum, espéculo

speech pathologist, foniatra

sperm, esperma

spermicide, espermicida

sphincter, esfínter

spider bite, picadura de araña

spina bifida, espina bífida

spinal column, columna vertebral

spinal cord, médula espinal

spleen, bazo

splint, férula

splint, entablillar

splinter, astilla

sponge, esponja

spots, manchas

spotted fever, fiebre maculosa

sprain, torcedura

My List of Key Medical Terms In Spanish

sprain, torcerse

sputum, esputo

stab, puñalada

stain, mancha

starvation, inanición

sterile, estéril

sterility, esterilidad

sterilize, esterilizar

sternum, esternón

steroid, esteroide

stethoscope, estetoscopio

stiff, rígido

stimulant, estimulante

sting, picadura de insecto

sting, picar

stirrup, estribo

stitches, puntos de suturas

stoma, estoma

stomach, estómago

stomach ache/pain, dolor de estómago

stool, excremento

strangle, estrangular

strength, fuerza

strep, estreptococo

stress, estrés

stretch mark, estría

stretcher, camilla

stroke, derrame cerebral

strong, fuerte

stuffy nose, nariz tapada

stupor, estupor

stutter, tartamudear

suffocation, sofocación

suicide, suicidio

sunburn, quemadura por el sol

sunstroke, insolación

suppository, supositorio

surgeon, cirujano

surgery, cirugía

surrogate mother, madre portadora

survive, sobrevivir

suture, sutura

swab, hisopo

swallow, tragar

sweat, sudor

swelling, hinchazón

swollen, hinchado

symptom, síntoma

syndrome, síndrome

synthetic, sintético

syphilis, sífilis

syringe, jeringa

syrup, jarabe

T

table, mesa
tablespoonful, cucharada
tablet, tableta
tailbone, cóccix
take, tomar
talcum powder, talco
tampon, tampón
tapeworm, teniasis
taste, sabor
taste bud, papila gustativa
tattoo, tatuaje
tear (of muscle/ligament), desgarro
tear (of the eye), lágrima
teaspoonful, cucharadita

My List of Key Medical Terms In Spanish

technician, técnico

temperature, temperatura

temple (of the head), sien

temporary, temporal

tender, adolorido

tendinitis, tendinitis

tendon, tendón

terminal, terminal

test, prueba/examen

testicles, testículos

testosterone, testosterona

tetanus, tétano

therapist, terapeuta

therapy, terapia

thermometer, termómetro

thick, espeso (consistency)/grueso (dimension)

thigh, muslo

thirst, sed

thirsty (to be), tener sed

thorax, tórax

throat, garganta

throbbing, pulsante

thrombosis, trombosis

throw up, vomitar

How Do You Say *Stomach* in Guatemala?

thumb, pulgar

thyroid gland, glándula tiroides

tincture, tintura

tingling, hormigueo

tinnitus, zumbido en los oídos

tissue, tejido

tobacco, tabaco

toe, dedo del pie

toilet, inodoro

tolerate, tolerar

tongue, lengua

tonic, tónico

tonsil, amígdala

tonsillectomy, amigdalectomía

tonsillitis, amigdalitis

tooth, diente

toothache, dolor de muelas

touch, tocar

tourniquet, torniquete

towel, toalla

toxemia, toxemia

toxic, tóxico

toxin, toxina

trace, rastro

My List of Key Medical Terms In Spanish

trachea, traquea

traction, tracción

tranquilizers, tranquilizantes

transfusion, transfusión

transmitted, transmitido

transplant, trasplantar

trauma, trauma

traumatic, traumático

treat, tratar

treatment, tratamiento

tremors, temblores

triceps, tríceps

trouble, molestia

tube, tubo

tuberculosis, tuberculosis

tumor, tumor

tweezers, pinzas

twin, gemelo

twisted, torcido

typhoid fever, fiebre tifoidea

typhus, tifus

U

ulcer, úlcera

ultrasound, ultrasonido

umbilical cord, cordón umbilical

uncomfortable, incómodo

unconscious, inconsciente

unhealthy, insalubre

unstable, inestable

urethra, uretra

urgent, urgente

urinal, orinal

urinalysis, examen general de orina

urinary, urinario

urinate, orinar

urine, orina

My List of Key Medical Terms In Spanish

urine sample, muestra de orina

urologist, urólogo

urology, urología

uterus, útero

V

vaccinate, vacunar
vaccine, vacuna
vagina, vagina
vaginal, vaginal
vaginitis, vaginitis
valve, válvula
varicose vein, vena varicosa
vascular, vascular
vasectomy, vasectomía
vegetative, vegetativo
vein, vena
venereal disease, enfermedad venérea
venom, veneno
ventilator, ventilador

My List of Key Medical Terms In Spanish

ventricle, ventrículo

vertebrae, vértebras

vertigo, vértigo

victim, víctima

virile, viril

virus, virus

vision, vista

visiting hours, horario de visita

vital, vital

vital organ, órgano vital

vital signs, signos vitales

vitamin, vitamina

vocal cord, cuerda vocal

vomit, vomitar

W

waist, cintura
waiting room, sala de espera
wake up, despertar
walker, andador
ward, sala
warning, aviso
wart, verruga
wash (to), lavar
water, agua
watery eyes, ojos llorosos
weak, débil
weakness, debilidad
wean, destetar
weary, fatigado

My List of Key Medical Terms In Spanish

weigh, pesar

weight, peso

weight change, cambio de peso

wet nurse, nodriza

wheel chair, silla de ruedas

wheeze, sibilancia

wheeze, respirar con sibilancias

white blood cells, glóbulos blancos

whooping cough (pertussis), tos ferina

windpipe, tráquea

wisdom tooth, muela del juicio

womb, útero

worms (intestinal), lombrices

wound, herida

wrist, muñeca

X

x-rays, radiografías/rayos X

Y

yawn, bostezar

SPANISH-ENGLISH
ESPAÑOL-INGLÉS

A

abdomen, abdomen

abdominal, abdominal

aborto, abortion

aborto natural, miscarriage

abrasión/raspadura, abrasion

absceso, abscess

abstinencia, abstinence

abuso, abuse

ácaro, mite

accidente, accident

acetaminofén, acetaminophen

acidez estomacal, heartburn

ácido, acid

ácido fólico, folic acid

My List of Key Medical Terms In Spanish

acné, acne

aconsejar, advise (to)

activo, active

adicción, addiction

adicción a las drogas, drug addiction

adicto, addict

adolescencia, adolescence

adolorido, tender

adoptar, adopt (to)

adormecimiento, numbness

adrenalina, adrenaline

adulto, adult

afligirse, grieve

agitación, agitation

agotamiento, exhaustion

agrandamiento, enlargement

agua, water

agudo, acute

agudo (dolor), sharp (pain)

aguja, needle

ahogamiento, drowning

ahogarse, choke

aire, air

alcoholismo, alcoholism

How Do You Say *Stomach* in Guatemala?

alergia, allergy
alérgico, allergic
aliento, breath
alimentar, feed
alimentos, food
alivio, relief
almohada, pillow
altura, height
alucinación, hallucination
amargo, bitter
ambulancia, ambulance
amenorrea, amenorrhea
amígdala, tonsil
amigdalectomía, tonsillectomy
amigdalitis, tonsillitis
aminoácido, amino acid
amnesia, amnesia
amniocentesis, amniocentesis
amoníaco, ammonia
amoratado, bruised
ampolla, blister
amputar, amputate (to)
analgésico, analgesic
análisis, analysis

My List of Key Medical Terms In Spanish

anatomía, anatomy

anciano, elderly

andador, walker

anemia, anemia

anémico, anemic

anestesia, anesthesia

anestesiólogo, anesthesiologist

aneurisma, aneurysm/aneurism

anfetaminas, amphetamines

angiograma, angiogram

angioplastia, angioplasty

angustiado, distressed

ano, anus

anorexia, anorexia

anormal, abnormal

anquilostomosis, hookworm

ansiedad, anxiety

antebrazo, forearm

antiácido, antacid

antibiótico, antibiotic

anticoagulante, anticoagulant

anticoncepción, contraception

anticuerpos, antibodies

antidepresivo, antidepressant

How Do You Say *Stomach* in Guatemala?

antídoto, antidote
antihistamínico, antihistamine
antojo, craving
ántrax, anthrax
aorta, aorta
aparato ortopédico, brace
apatía, apathy
apendectomía, appendectomy
apendicitis, appendicitis
apetito, appetite
aplicador, applicator
apnea, apnea
arrastrar las palabras, slur
arritmia, arrhythmia
arteria, artery
articulación, joint
artritis, arthritis
asfixia, asphyxia
asma, asthma
asmático, asthmatic
astigmatismo, astigmatism
astilla, sliver
astilla, splinter
ataque cardíaco, heart attack

My List of Key Medical Terms In Spanish

atención a la salud, health care

atrofia, atrophy

aturdimiento, daze

audición, hearing

autismo, autism

autopsia, autopsy

aviso, warning

axila, arm pit

ayunar, fast

B

babero, bib

bacteria, bacteria

balanza, scale

bañarse, bathe (to)

baño, bath

barbilla, chin

barbitúricos, barbiturates

bario, barium

bastón, cane

bata, gown

bazo, spleen

bebé, baby

bebé, infant

benigno, benign

My List of Key Medical Terms In Spanish

bíceps, biceps

bicúspide, bicuspid

bilirrubina, bilirubin

bilis, bile

biológico, biological

biopsia, biopsy

bizco, cross-eyed

boca, mouth

boca abajo, face down

boca arriba, face up

bocio, goiter

bolsa amniótica, amniotic sac

bomba, pump

borracho, drunk

bostezar, yawn

botella, bottle

botulismo, botulism

brazo, arm

bronquitis, bronchitis

bulimia, bulimia

bulímico, bulimic

bulto, lump

bursitis, bursitis

C

cabestrillo, sling

cabeza, head

cadera, hip

caída, fall

calambre, cramp

calcificado, calcified

calcio, calcium

cálculos biliares, gallstones

cálculos renales, kidney stones

callo, callus

callo, corn (callus)

calmante para el dolor, pain reliever

caloría, calorie

calvicie, baldness

My List of Key Medical Terms In Spanish

calvo, bald

cama, bed

cambio de peso, weight change

camilla, gurney

camilla, stretcher

cáncer, cancer

canceroso, cancerous

capilar, capillary

cápsula, capsule

cara, face

carbohidrato, carbohydrate

carcinogénico, carcinogenic

carcinoma, carcinoma

cardíaco, cardiac

cardiología, cardiology

cardiólogo, cardiologist

cartílago, cartilage

caspa, dandruff

castración, castration

catarata, cataract

catatónico, catatonic

catéter, catheter

cateterismo, catheterization

cateterizar, catheterize

How Do You Say *Stomach* in Guatemala?

causa, cause

cauterizar, cauterize

ceceo, lisp

ceguera, blindness

ceja, eyebrow

cerebro, brain

choque, shock

cicatriz, scar

ciclo menstrual, menstrual cycle

ciego, blind

cigarrillo, cigarette

cintura, waist

circulación, circulation

circuncisión, circumcision

cirrosis, cirrhosis

cirugía, surgery

cirujano, surgeon

cita, appointment

clamidia, chlamydia

claustrofobia, claustrophobia

clavícula, collarbone

clínica, clinic

clítoris, clitoris

coágulo, clot

cocaína, cocaine
cóccix, coccyx
cóccix, tailbone
codeína, codeine
codo, elbow
cojín eléctrico, heating pad
colágeno, collagen
cólera, cholera
colesterol, cholesterol
cólico, colic
cólicos menstruales, cramps (menstrual)
colitis, colitis
colon, colon
colonoscopía, colonoscopy
colostomia, colostomy
columna vertebral, backbone
columna vertebral, spinal column
coma, coma
comatoso, comatose
comezón, itch
cómodo, comfortable
complicación, complication
compresa, compress
concebir, conceive

How Do You Say *Stomach* in Guatemala?

condón, condom
conducta, behavior
confundido, confused
confusión, confusion
congelar, freeze
congénito, congenital
congestión, congestion
conjuntiva, conjunctiva
conjuntivitis, conjunctivitis
conmoción cerebral, concussion
conocimiento, consciousness
consciente, conscious
consentir, consent
consultorio, doctor's office
consultorio, office
contagioso, contagious
contaminado, contaminated
contracciones, contractions
contusión, contusion
convaleciente, convalescent
convulsión, convulsion
convulsiones, seizures
corazón, heart
cordón umbilical, umbilical cord

cordura, sanity
coronario, coronary
cortar, cut
cortisona, cortisone
costilla, rib
costra, scab
cráneo, cranium
cráneo, skull
crecimiento, growth
crítico, critical
crónico, chronic
crup, croup
cuádriceps, quadriceps
cuarentena, quarantine
cucharada, tablespoonful
cucharadita, teaspoonful
cuchillo, knife
cuello, neck
cuello del útero, cervix
cuerda vocal, vocal cord
cuerdo, sane
cuero cabelludo, scalp
cuerpo, body
cuidado, care

How Do You Say *Stomach* in Guatemala?

cuidado prenatal, prenatal care

culpa, guilt

cultivo, culture

cuna, crib

cuota, quota

curandero, folk healer

curar, cure

curarse, heal

curita, bandaid

cutícula, cuticle

CH

chupete, pacifier

ciática, sciatica

D

daltonismo, color-blindness
dañado, impaired
dañar, harm
dañino, harmful
dar de alta, discharge from hospital
débil, weak
debilidad, weakness
dedo (de la mano), finger
dedo del pie, toe
defecar, defecate
deficiencia, deficiency
deformado, deformed
deformidad, deformity
delirante, delirious

My List of Key Medical Terms In Spanish

delirio, delirium

deltoides, deltoids

demencia, dementia

dentadura postiza, denture

dental, dental

dentista, dentist

depresión, depression

dermatitis, dermatitis

dermatólogo, dermatologist

derrame cerebral, stroke

desarrollar, develop

descansar, relax

descansar, rest

descongestionante, decongestant

deseo sexual, libido

desfibrilación, defibrillation

desfibrilador, defibrillator

desgarro, tear (of muscle/ligament)

deshidratación, dehydration

desinfectante, disinfectant

desinfectar, disinfect

desintoxicación, detoxification

desmayarse, faint

desmayos, fainting spells

desnudo, naked

desnutrición, malnutrition

desorientación, disorientation

despertar, awaken (to)

despertar, wake up

despierto, awake

despigmentación, depigmentation

después de la operación, post-op

destetar, wean

deterioro, deterioration

diabetes, diabetes

diafragma, diaphragm

diagnosticar, diagnose

diagnóstico, diagnosis

diálisis, dialysis

diariamente, daily

diarrea, diarrhea

diente, tooth

diente impactado, impacted tooth

dientes postizos, false teeth

dieta, diet

dietista, dietitian

difteria, diphtheria

difunto, deceased

My List of Key Medical Terms In Spanish

digerir, digest
digestión, digestion
dilatación, dilation
dilatado, dilated
diluir, dilute
discapacidad, disability
disco desplazado, disk (slipped)
disco desplazado, slipped disc
disentería, dysentery
dislexia, dyslexia
dislocación, dislocation
distender, distend
distrofia, dystrophy
diurético, diuretic
doler, hurt
dolor, ache
dolor, pain
dolor de cabeza, headache
dolor de estómago, stomach ache/pain
dolor de muelas, toothache
dolor de oído, earache
dolores de parto, labor pains
doloroso, painful
donante, donor

How Do You Say *Stomach* in Guatemala?

dormir, sleep

dosis, dosage

drogas, drugs (usually illicit)

duodeno, duodenum

E

eccema, eczema
ecografía, sonogram
edema, edema
edema pulmonar, pulmonary edema
efecto secundario, side effect
ejercicio, exercise
electrocardiograma, EKG
electrocardiograma, electrocardiogram
electrocución, electrocution
elixir, elixir
embarazada, pregnant
embarazo, pregnancy
embolia, embolism
embrión, embryo

How Do You Say *Stomach* in Guatemala?

emergencia, emergency

empaste, filling (dental)

enanismo, dwarfism

encamado, bedridden (patient)

encefalitis, encephalitis

encías, gums

endémico, endemic

endocrino, endocrine

endocrinólogo, endocrinologist

endorfina, endorphin

endoscopía, endoscopy

endurecimiento, hardening

enema, enema

enfermedad, ailment

enfermedad, disease

enfermedad, illness

enfermedad, sickness

enfermedad de Crohn, Crohn's disease

enfermedad venérea, venereal disease

enfermera, nurse

enfermo, ill

enfermo, sick

enfisema pulmonar, pulmonary emphysema

enojo, anger

My List of Key Medical Terms In Spanish

enrojecimiento, redness
entablillar, splint
enuresis, bed-wetting
enzima, enzyme
epidémico/epidemia, epidemic
epidural, epidural
epiglotis, epiglottis
epilepsia, epilepsy
equilibrio, balance
erección, erection
eructar, burp
eructo, belch
erupción, rash
escaldadura, scald
escalofríos, chills
escalofríos, shiver
escama, flake
escamoso, scaly
escoliosis, scoliosis
escorbuto, scurvy
escroto, scrotum
escuálido, emaciated
escuchar, listen
esfínter, sphincter

How Do You Say *Stomach* in Guatemala?

esfuerzo, exertion

esófago, esophagus

espalda, back

espasmo, spasm

especialista, specialist

espéculo, speculum

esperma, sperm

espermicida, spermicide

espeso (consistency)/grueso (dimension), thick

espina bífida, spina bifida

espinilla, shin

espinillas, blackheads

espinillas, pimples

esponja, sponge

espuma, foam

esputo, sputum

esqueleto, skeleton

esquizofrenia, schizophrenia

estar congestionado, congested (to be)

estéril, infertile

estéril, sterile

esterilidad, sterility

esterilizar, sterilize

esternón, breastbone

My List of Key Medical Terms In Spanish

esternón, sternum
esteroide, steroid
estetoscopio, stethoscope
estilo de vida, lifestyle
estimulante, stimulant
estoma, stoma
estómago, stomach
estornudar, sneeze
estrangular, strangle
estreñimiento, constipation
estreptococo, strep
estrés, stress
estría, stretch mark
estribo, stirrup
estrógeno, estrogen
estupor, stupor
éter, ether
euforia, euphoria
eutanasia, euthanasia
examen, checkup
examen, exam
examen de detección, screen
examen de Papanicolaou, Pap smear
examen de seguimiento, follow-up

examen general de orina, urinalysis

examinar, examine

excremento, excrement

excremento, stool

exfoliación, exfoliation

exhalar, exhale

expectorante, expectorant

expediente médico, medical record

experto, expert

explicar, explain

exposición, exposure

externo, external

extracción, extraction

extraer, extract

extremidad, limb

extremidad lisiada, lame extremity

eyacular, ejaculate

F

faringe, pharynx

farmacéutico, pharmacist

farmacia, pharmacy

fatal/mortal, fatal

fatiga, fatigue

fatigado, weary

fecha aproximada de parto, due date

fecundación, impregnation

fémur, femur

fértil, fertile

fertilización, fertilization

férula, splint

feto, fetus

fibra, fiber

fibrilación, fibrillation

fibrosis quística, cystic fibrosis

fiebre, fever

fiebre escarlatina, scarlet fever

fiebre maculosa, spotted fever

fiebre reumática, rheumatic fever

fiebre tifoidea, typhoid fever

fisioterapia, physical therapy

fisura, fissure

flaco, skinny

flatulencia, flatulence

flema, phlegm

flexible, flexible

fluoruro, fluoride

fobia, phobia

folículo, follicle

foniatra, speech pathologist

fórceps, forceps

fórmula, formula

formulario, form

fosa nasal, nostril

fósforo, phosphorus

fotosensibilidad, photosensitivity

fractura, fracture

My List of Key Medical Terms In Spanish

frecuencia, frequency

frenos dentales, braces (dental)

frente, forehead

frío/a, cold

fuego/incendio, fire

fuerte, strong

fuerza, strength

fumar, smoke

función, function

G

gafas, glasses

ganglios linfáticos, lymph nodes

gangrena, gangrene

garganta, throat

gas, gas

gas hilarante (óxido nitroso), laughing gas

gasa, gauze

gastritis, gastritis

gastroenterólogo, gastroenterologist

gastrointestinal, gastrointestinal (GI)

gatear, crawl

gel, gel

gemelo, twin

genes, genes

genético, genetic
genitales, genitals
geriátrico, geriatric
germen, germ
gestación, gestation
giardia, giardia
gigantismo, gigantism
ginecología, gynecology
ginecólogo, gynecologist
gingivitis, gingivitis
glándula, gland
glándula tiroides, thyroid gland
glaucoma, glaucoma
glóbulos blancos, white blood cells
glucosa, glucose
gluten, gluten
glúteo, buttock
gonorrea, gonorrhea
gordo, fat (person)
gota, gout
gotas, drops
gotero, dropper
gramo, gram
grasa, fat (food)

How Do You Say *Stomach* in Guatemala?

gripe, flu

gripe, influenza

grito, scream

guante, glove

H

hábito, habit

hacer gárgaras, gargle

heces, feces

helicóptero, helicopter

hematoma, hematoma

hemofilia, hemophilia

hemoglobina, hemoglobin

hemorragia, hemorrhage

hepatitis, hepatitis

hereditario, hereditary

herencia, heredity

herida, wound

hermafrodita, hermaphrodite

hermano/hermana, sibling

How Do You Say *Stomach* in Guatemala?

hernia, hernia
heroína, heroin
herpes, herpes
herpes labial, cold sores
herpes zoster, shingles
heterosexual, heterosexual
hidratar, hydrate
hierba, herb
hierro, iron
hígado, liver
higiene, hygiene
himen, hymen
hinchado, swollen
hinchazón, swelling
hiperactivo, hyperactive
hiperglucemia, hyperglycemia
hipersensibilidad, hypersensitivity
hipertermia, hyperthermia
hipertiroidismo, hyperthyroidism
hiperventilación, hyperventilation
hipo, hiccups
hipocondria, hypochondria
hipoglucemia, hypoglycemia
hipotálamo, hypothalamus

My List of Key Medical Terms In Spanish

hipotermia, hypothermia

hipotiroidismo, hypothyroidism

hipoxia, hypoxia

hisopo, swab

histerectomía, hysterectomy

histeria, hysteria

hombro, shoulder

homeopatía, homeopathy

homosexual, homosexual

hongo, fungus

horario de visita, visiting hours

hormigueo, tingling

hormona, hormone

hormonal, hormonal

hospital, hospital

hueso, bone

huevo/óvulo, egg

I

ibuprofeno, ibuprofen

ictericia/piel amarilla, jaundice

implantar, implant

impotencia, impotence

inanición, starvation

incapacidad, impairment

incesto, incest

incisión, incision

incómodo, uncomfortable

inconsciente, unconscious

incontinencia, incontinence

incubadora, incubator

incurable, incurable

indigestión, indigestion

My List of Key Medical Terms In Spanish

inducir, induce

inestable, unstable

infancia, childhood

infección, infection

infectar, infect

infertilidad, infertility

inflamación, inflammation

ingerir, ingest

ingle, groin

ingresar, admit (into hospital)

inhalador, inhaler

inhalar, inhale

injerto, graft

inmaduro, immature

inmóvil, immobile

inmovilización, immobilization

inmune, immune

inmunizar, immunize

inoculación, inoculation

inocular, inoculate

inodoro, toilet

inofensivo, harmless

insalubre, unhealthy

inseminación, insemination

How Do You Say *Stomach* in Guatemala?

insolación, heat-stroke
insolación, sunstroke
insomnio, insomnia
instrumento, instrument
insuficiencia renal, kidney failure
insuficiencia renal, renal failure
insulina, insulin
internar, hospitalize
internista, internist
interno, internal
intestino, bowel
intestino, intestine
intestino delgado, small intestine
intestino grueso, large intestine
intestino/tripas, gut
intoxicación, intoxication
intubación, intubation
inyección, shot
inyectar, inject
irrigar, irrigate
irritación, irritation

J

jabón, soap

jalea, jelly

jarabe, syrup

jeringa, syringe

jorobado, hunchback

juanete, bunion

jugo, juice

L

laberintitis, labyrinthitis

labios, lips

laboratorio, laboratory

laceración, laceration

lactancia, lactation

lactosa, lactose

ladillas, crabs

lado, side

lágrima, tear (of the eye)

laparoscopía, laparoscopy

laringe, larynx

laringitis, laryngitis

látex, latex

latido del corazón, heartbeat

latidos cardíacos irregulares, irregular heartbeat

My List of Key Medical Terms In Spanish

lavar, wash (to)
laxante, laxative
lengua, tongue
lenguaje, language
lepra, leprosy
lesbiana, lesbian
lesión, injury
lesión, lesion
letargo, lethargy
leucemia, leukemia
libra, pound
ligamento, ligament
linfa, lymph
linfoma, lymphoma
linimento, liniment
liposucción, liposuction
líquido, liquid
líquidos intravenosos, intravenous fluids
lisiado, crippled
lisiar, cripple
llaga, sore
llorar, cry
lobotomía, lobotomy
lóbulo, earlobe

How Do You Say *Stomach* in Guatemala?

lóbulo, lobe

loco, insane

locura, insanity

lombrices, worms (intestinal)

lubricar, lubricate

lunar, birthmark

lunar, mole

lupus, lupus

M

madre portadora, surrogate mother

madurez, maturity

mal aliento, halitosis

malabsorción, malabsorption

malestar, malaise

malformación, malformation

maligno, malignant

malo(a), bad

mamografía, mammogram

mancha, stain

manchas, spots

mandíbula, jaw

manía, mania

maníaco depresivo, manic-depressive

mano, hand

How Do You Say *Stomach* in Guatemala?

marcapaso, pacemaker

mareado, dizzy

mareo (en un barco), seasickness

mareos, dizziness

marihuana, marijuana

martillo de reflejos, hammer

masa, mass

masajear, massage/rub

máscara, mask

mastectomía, mastectomy

masticar, chew

materno, maternal

medicamento, medication

medicina, medicine

medicinas, drugs (legal)

médico, doctor

médico, physician

médula espinal, spinal cord

mejilla, cheek

melanoma, melanoma

meningitis, meningitis

menopausia, menopause

menstruación, menses

menstruación, menstruation

My List of Key Medical Terms In Spanish

mente, mind

mesa, table

metabolismo, metabolism

metadona, methadone

metanfetamina, methamphetamine

metástasis, metastasis

método del ritmo, rhythm method

microcirugía, microsurgery

microscopio, microscope

miedo, fear

migraña, migraine

miopía, myopia

miopía, nearsightedness

moler, grind

molestia, trouble

monitor, monitor

monitor fetal, fetal monitor

mononucleosis, mononucleosis

mordedura, bite

mordedura de serpiente, snakebite

moretón, bruise

morfina, morphine

morgue, morgue

morir, die

mortalidad, mortality

mucoso/mucosa, mucous

mudo, mute

muela del juicio, wisdom tooth

muerte, death

muerto, dead

muestra, sample

muestra de orina, urine sample

muestra/espécimen, specimen

muletas, crutches

muñeca, wrist

músculo, muscle

músculo posterior del muslo, hamstring

muslo, thigh

mutación, mutation

N

nacimiento prematuro, premature birth
nacimiento/parto, birth
narcolepsia, narcolepsy
narcótico, narcotic
nariz, nose
nariz tapada, stuffy nose
natural, natural
náuseas, nausea
negligencia médica, malpractice
nervio, nerve
nervioso, nervous
neuralgia, neuralgia
neurología, neurology
neurólogo, neurologist
neurosis, neurosis

neurótico, neurotic

nicotina, nicotine

nitroglicerina, nitroglycerine

nodriza, wet nurse

normal, normal

nuca, nape

nudillo, knuckle

nudo, knot

nutrición, nourishment

nutrición, nutrition

nutricionista, nutritionist

nutriente, nutrient

O

obesidad, obesity

obeso, obese

obstetra, obstetrician

obstetricia, obstetrics

obstrucción, blockage

obstrucción, obstruction

oclusión, occlusion

oftalmólogo, ophthalmologist

oído, ear (inner)

oído medio, ear (middle)

oír, hear

ojo, eye

ojos llorosos, watery eyes

oler, smell

olor, odor

How Do You Say *Stomach* in Guatemala?

ombligo, bellybutton
ombligo, navel
omóplato, shoulder blade
oncología, oncology
oncólogo, oncologist
operar, operate
óptico, optic
optometrista, optometrist
oral, oral
oreja, ear (outer)
órgano, organ
órgano vital, vital organ
orgasmo, orgasm
orina, urine
orinal, bedpan
orinal, urinal
orinar, urinate
ortodoncista, orthodontist
ortopedia, orthopedics
ortopedista, orthopedist
osteoartritis, osteoarthritis
osteópata, osteopath
osteoporosis, osteoporosis
ovario, ovary

ovulación, ovulation

ovular, ovulate

oxígeno, oxygen

P

paciente, patient

padrastro, hangnail

paladar, palate

paladar hendido, cleft palate

palangana, basin

palidez, paleness

pálido, pale

palpitaciones, palpitations

paludismo, malaria

páncreas, pancreas

pantorilla, calf (of leg)

pañal, diaper

paperas, mumps

papila gustativa, taste bud

parálisis, paralysis

My List of Key Medical Terms In Spanish

paralítico, paralyzed

paramédico, paramedic

paranoia, paranoia

parapléjico, paraplegic

parásito, parasite

parche, patch

parentesco, relationship (family)

parpadear, blink

párpado, eyelid

partera, midwife

parto, childbirth

parto, delivery (of a baby)

pastillas para la garganta, lozenges

paterno, paternal

patólogo, pathologist

peca, freckle

pecho, chest

pecho/seno, breast/chest

pediatra, pediatrician

pediatría, pediatrics

pediátrico, pediatric

peligro, danger

pelo, hair

pelvis, pelvis

How Do You Say *Stomach* in Guatemala?

pene, penis
penetrar, penetrate
penicilina, penicillin
perforación, perforation
peróxido de hidrógeno, hydrogen peroxide
pesadilla, nightmare
pesar, grief
pesar, weigh
peso, weight
pestaña, eyelash
pezón, nipple
picadura, bite (insect)
picadura de araña, spider bite
picadura de insecto, sting
picar, sting
pie, foot
pie de atleta, athlete's foot
pie plano, flat foot
piel, skin
piel de gallina, goose bumps
pierna, leg
pies, feet
píldora, pill
pinzas, tweezers

My List of Key Medical Terms In Spanish

piojos, lice

pistola, gun

placa, plaque

placenta, afterbirth

placenta, placenta

plaga, plague

planificación familiar, family planning

planta del pie, sole (of foot)

plaquetas, platelets

plasma, plasma

plomo, lead

podólogo, podiatrist

polen, pollen

poliomielitis, polio

pólipo, polyp

polvo, dust

polvo, powder

poro, pore

posparto, postpartum

postmenopáusico, postmenopausal

potasio, potassium

pre eclampsia, preeclampsia

pre menopáusico, premenopausal

predisponer, predispose

prepucio, foreskin
presión, pressure
presión alta, high blood pressure
presión alta, hypertension
presión baja, low blood pressure
prevención, prevention
prevenir, prevent
primeros auxilios, first aid
procedimiento, procedure
proctólogo, proctologist
progesterona, progesterone
pronóstico, prognosis
próstata, prostate gland
proteína, protein
protuberancia, bump
provocar náuseas, gag
prueba/examen, test
psicólogo, psychologist
psicosis, psychosis
psicoterapia, psychotherapy
psicótico, psychotic
psiquiatra, psychiatrist
psoriasis, psoriasis
pubertad, puberty

My List of Key Medical Terms In Spanish

pulgar, thumb

pulmonar, pulmonary

pulmones, lungs

pulmonía, pneumonia

pulsante, pulsating

pulsante, throbbing

pulso, pulse

puntos de suturas, stitches

puñalada, stab

puño, fist

pupila, pupil

pus, pus

Q

quebrar, break

queja, complaint

quemadura, burn

quemadura por el sol, sunburn

químico, chemical

quimioterapia, chemotherapy

quinina, quinine

quiropráctico, chiropractor

quiste, cyst

R

rabia, rabies

radiografías/rayos X, x-rays

radiología, radiology

radiólogo, radiologist

radioterapia, radiotherapy

rasguño, scratch

rastro, trace

reacción, reaction

reanimación cardiopulmonar, CPR

reanimarse, revive

recaída, relapse

receta, prescription

recetar, prescribe

rechazar, reject

reconstruir, reconstruct

How Do You Say *Stomach* in Guatemala?

recto, rectum

recuperación, recovery

reemplazar, replace

reflejo, reflex

reflujo, reflux

regurgitación, regurgitation

rehabilitar, rehabilitate

rehidratar, rehydrate

relaciones sexuales, intercourse

rellenar, refill

remedio, remedy

reproducción, reproduction

reproducir, reproduce

resaca, hangover

resbalar, slip

resfriado común, cold (illness)

respirador, respirator

respirar, breathe

respirar con sibilancias, wheeze

respiratorio, respiratory

resucitación, resuscitation

resultado, result

retención, retention

retina, retina

reumatismo, rheumatism

riesgo, risk

rigidez, rigidity

rígido, stiff

rigor mortis, rigor mortis

rinoplastia, rhinoplasty

riñón, kidney

rodilla, knee

roncar, snore

ronchas, hives

ronco, hoarse

ronquera, hoarseness

roto, broken

rótula, kneecap

rozar, chafe

rubéola, German measles

rubéola, rubella

rubor, flush

ruptura, rupture

S

sabor, taste

sacar sangre, draw blood

sal, salt

sala, ward

sala de espera, waiting room

salino, saline

saliva, saliva

salmonela, salmonella

salud, health

sangrar, bleed

sangre, blood

sanguijuela, leech

sanitario, sanitary

sano, healthy

sarampión, measles

sarcoma, sarcoma

sarna, scabies

secreción, discharge

secreción, secretion

secreción nasal, runny nose

secretar, secrete

sed, thirst

sedante, sedative

sedentario, sedentary

seguro, insurance

seguro, safe

sellador, sealant

semen, semen

senil, senile

senilidad, senility

seno paranasal, sinus

sensación, sensation

sensibilidad, sensitivity

sensible, sensitive

sentir, feel

sequedad, dryness

serio, serious

severo, severe

sexo, gender

How Do You Say *Stomach* in Guatemala?

sexo, sex

sexualidad, sexuality

shock anafiláctico, anaphylactic

sibilancia, wheeze

sien, temple (of the head)

siesta, nap

sífilis, syphilis

signos vitales, vital signs

silla de ruedas, wheel chair

síndrome, syndrome

sintético, synthetic

síntoma, symptom

sinusitis, sinusitis

sobredosis, overdose

sobrepeso, overweight

sobrevivir, survive

sobrio, sober

sodio, sodium

sofocación, suffocation

sofocos, hot flashes

somnífero, sleeping pill

somnoliento, drowsy

sordera, deafness

sordo, deaf

sordo (dolor), dull (pain)

sordomudo, deaf-mute

subir de peso, gain weight

sudor, sweat

suero, serum

suicidio, suicide

supositorio, suppository

supurar, drain

suspender, discontinue

susto, fright

sutura, suture

T

tabaco, tobacco

tabique, septum

tableta, tablet

tajo, gash

talco, talcum powder

talón, heel

tampón, tampon

tapones para los oídos, earplugs

tartamudear, stutter

tatuaje, tattoo

técnico, technician

tejido, tissue

temblores, shakes

temblores, tremors

temperatura, temperature

My List of Key Medical Terms In Spanish

temporal, temporary

tendinitis, tendinitis

tendón, tendon

tener sed, thirsty (to be)

tener sueño, sleepy

teniasis, tapeworm

terapeuta, therapist

terapia, therapy

terapia intensiva, intensive care

terminal, terminal

termómetro, thermometer

testículos, testicles

testosterona, testosterone

tétano, tetanus

tétanos, lockjaw

tez, complexion

tifus, typhus

tijeras, scissors

tímpano, eardrum

tintura, tincture

tiña crural, jock itch

tiritar, shiver

toalla, towel

tocar, touch

How Do You Say *Stomach* in Guatemala?

tolerar, tolerate
tomar, take
tomografía por computadora, CT scan
tónico, tonic
tórax, thorax
torcedura, sprain
torcerse, sprain
torcido, twisted
torniquete, tourniquet
tos, cough
tos ferina, pertussis
tos ferina, whooping cough (pertussis)
toser, cough
toxemia, toxemia
tóxico, toxic
toxina, toxin
trabajador social, social worker
trabajo de parto, labor
tracción, traction
tragar, swallow
tranquilizantes, tranquilizers
transfusión, transfusion
transmitido, transmitted
transpirar, perspire

traquea, trachea

tráquea, windpipe

trasplantar, transplant

trastorno, disorder

trastorno mental, mental illness

tratamiento, treatment

tratamiento con láser, laser treatment

tratamiento de radiación, radiation treatment

tratar, treat

trauma, trauma

traumático, traumatic

tríceps, triceps

trombosis, thrombosis

trompa de Eustaquio, Eustachian tube

trompas de Falopio, Fallopian tubes

tuberculosis, tuberculosis

tubo, tube

tumor, tumor

tumorectomía, lumpectomy

U

úlcera, ulcer

úlcera gástrica, gastric ulcer

ultrasonido, ultrasound

ungüento, ointment

uña, nail

uretra, urethra

urgente, urgent

urinario, urinary

urología, urology

urólogo, urologist

útero, uterus

útero, womb

V

vacuna, vaccine

vacuna de refuerzo, booster shot

vacunar, vaccinate

vagina, vagina

vaginal, vaginal

vaginitis, vaginitis

vahído, light-headedness

válvula, valve

varicela, chicken pox

varón/masculino, male

vascular, vascular

vasectomía, vasectomy

vegetativo, vegetative

vejiga, bladder

vello, hair (body)

How Do You Say *Stomach* in Guatemala?

vello púbico, pubic hair

vena, vein

vena varicosa, varicose vein

vendaje, bandage

veneno, poison

veneno, venom

ventilador, ventilator

ventrículo, ventricle

verruga, wart

vértebras, vertebrae

vértigo, vertigo

vesícula biliar, gall bladder

víctima, victim

vida, life

vientre, belly

violación, rape

viril, virile

viruela, smallpox

virus, virus

vista, eyesight

vista, sight

vista, vision

vista doble, double vision

vital, vital

My List of Key Medical Terms In Spanish

vitamina, vitamin

vivir, live

vivo, alive

vomitar, throw up

vomitar, vomit

Y

yema, finger pad

yerbero, herbalist

yeso, cast

yodo, iodine

yugular, jugular

Z

zumbido, buzzing

zumbido en los oídos, tinnitus

zurdo, left-handed

ABOUT THE AUTHOR

For more than 25 years, José Luis Leyva has worked as a translator and interpreter in various technical areas, including medical environments. His vast experience in bilingualism has allowed him to interpret for directors of medical institutions, prosecutors, forensic experts, specialists and health professionals. He is also the author of other books, including technical dictionaries of the ***How Do You Say?*** series.